DATE DUE

OCT 16 2017			
			PRINTED IN U.S.A.

Amicus Illustrated is published by Amicus
P.O. Box 1329, Mankato, MN 56002
www.amicuspublishing.us

This library-bound edition is reprinted by arrangement with Chronicle Books LLC, 680 Second Street, San Francisco, California 94107.

First published in the United States in 2004 by Chronicle Books LLC.

Adaptation © 1993 by Francesc Boada.
Illustrations © 1993 by Pau Estrada.
Spanish/English text © 2004 by Chronicle Books LLC.
Originally published in Catalan in 1994 by La Galera, S.A. Editorial.
All rights reserved.

Bilingual version supervised by SUR Editorial Group, Inc.
English translation by Arshes Anasal.
Book design by Alison Dacher.
Typeset in Weiss and Handle Oldstyle.

Library of Congress Cataloging-in-Publication Data
Boada, Francesc.
[Princesa i el pèsol. English & Spanish]
 The princess and the pea = La princesa y el guisante / adaptation by Francesc Boada ; illustrated by Pau Estrada.
     p. cm. — (Bilingual fairy tales)
"Originally published in Catalan in 1994 by La Galera, S.A. Editorial."
 Summary: By feeling a pea through twenty mattresses and twenty featherbeds, a girl proves that she is a real princess.
 ISBN 978-1-60753-357-3 (library binding)
[1. Fairy tales. 2. Spanish language materials--Bilingual.] I. Estrada, Pau, ill. II. Andersen, H. C. (Hans Christian), 1805-1875. Prindsessen paa ærten. III. Title. IV. Title: Princesa y el guisante.
 PZ73.B62313 2014
 [E]—dc23   2012041712

Printed in the United States of America at Corporate Graphics Inc, North Mankato, Minnesota.
1-2013/PO1155
10 9 8 7 6 5 4 3 2 1

THE PRINCESS AND THE PEA

LA PRINCESA Y EL GUISANTE

ADAPTATION BY FRANCESC BOADA
ILLUSTRATED BY PAU ESTRADA

amicus
illustrated

Once upon a time there was a prince who wished to marry a princess. But he wanted to be sure she was a *true* princess.

~

Había una vez un príncipe que quería casarse con una princesa. Pero quería estar seguro de que fuese una princesa *de verdad*.

So the prince climbed onto his horse and set out across the world to find a true princess to marry.

～

El príncipe montó en su caballo y marchó a correr mundo buscando una princesa de verdad para casarse con ella.

He traveled to many lands. There were many princesses, but it was so difficult to know if they were true princesses! There was always something that didn't seem quite right.

～

Recorrió muchas tierras. Princesas, había muchas … pero ¡qué difícil era saber si eran princesas de verdad! Siempre les encontraba algún defecto.

So without a bride, the prince returned to his palace sad and discouraged.

~

Sin haber conseguido novia, el príncipe regresó a su palacio triste y desanimado.

One night, there was a terrible rainstorm. The wind howled and water poured down in torrents. The thunder boomed and lightning crackled in the sky.

In the midst of all this, there was a knock at the palace door. The king himself went down to see who was there.

Una tarde se desató una tormenta terrible, con unos relámpagos y unos truenos que asustaban. El viento aullaba, y el agua caía a cántaros.

En medio de la tormenta, alguien llamó a la puerta del palacio, y el propio rey bajó a abrir.

The king couldn't believe his eyes. Standing before him was a shivering princess drenched by the storm. Water cascaded down her hair and dress and came out of her shoes. She was so wet she looked more like a fountain than a princess.

But in spite of all this, she claimed to be a *true* princess.

El rey no pudo creer en lo que veía. Había una princesa, empapada y temblando de frío frente a él. El agua le chorreaba por el pelo y por el vestido, y le salía por los zapatos. Estaba tan mojada que más que una princesa parecía una fuente.

Pero a pesar de todo esto, afirmó ser una princesa *de verdad*.

When the queen heard the news, she thought, "Very soon we'll know if she is a true princess."

Without telling anyone, the queen went up to a bedroom and placed a pea on the bed. Then she covered the pea with twenty mattresses filled with wool and twenty mattresses filled with feathers.

The princess spent the night in this very tall bed.

⁓

Al enterarse, la reina pensó: "Enseguida sabremos si es una princesa de verdad."

Y sin decirle a nadie, subió al dormitorio y colocó un guisante sobre la cama. Encima del guisante puso veinte colchones de lana y veinte de plumas.

La princesa pasó la noche en esa cama tan alta.

The next day, the queen asked the princess how she had slept.

"Very poorly," answered the princess. "I hardly slept at all. There was a terrible lump in the mattress, and now I'm covered with bruises. What a night!"

—

Al día siguiente, la reina le preguntó cómo había dormido.

—¡Oh, muy mal! —respondió la princesa—. No he podido pegar un ojo en toda la noche. Había algo duro en el colchón que me ha dejado cubierta de moretones. ¡Qué noche!

On hearing this, the queen realized the princess was indeed a *true* princess. In spite of the twenty wool mattresses and the twenty feather mattresses, she had been uncomfortable because of the pea.

As everybody knows, only a true princess could be so delicate.

Al oír esto, la reina comprobó que la princesa era realmente una princesa *de verdad*. Porque a pesar de los veinte colchones de lana y de veinte más de plumas, ella había sentido las molestias del guisante.

Como todo el mundo sabe, sólo una princesa de verdad puede ser tan delicada.

So the prince and the princess married.

～

Y el príncipe y la princesa se casaron.

As for the pea, it was taken to a museum, and probably it is still there, unless someone ate it.

~

El guisante … lo llevaron a un museo. Y allí debe estar aún si es que alguien no se lo ha comido.

Pau Estrada is a native of Barcelona, Spain, where he studied literature. In 1986 he received a Fulbright scholarship for graduate studies at Rhode Island School of Design. He has since illustrated many children's books for publishers in the United States and in Spain. Apart from teaching and illustrating, his interests include music, travel, and multimedia.

Pau Estrada nació en Barcelona, España, donde estudió literatura. En 1986 recibió una beca Fulbright para continuar sus estudios en Estados Unidos, en Rhode Island School of Design. Desde entonces ha ilustrado varios libros infantiles para editoriales en España y Estados Unidos. Además de la enseñanza y la ilustración, Pau Estrada también se dedica a la música, a viajar y al video-arte.

Also in this series:

Cinderella ✦ Beauty and the Beast ✦ The Princess and the Pea
Puss in Boots ✦ Rapunzel ✦ Rumpelstiltskin

También en esta serie:

Cenicienta ✦ La bella y la bestia ✦ La princesa y el guisante
El gato con botas ✦ Rapunzel ✦ Rumpelstiltskin